MGIS SYSTEMS NETWORKS AND CODES

Mgis.ask.davidgomadza.start.whatis.start

David Gomadza

President Tomorrow's World Order

Yahweh's Representative on Earth

www.twofuture.world

Copyright © 2024 David Gomadza

All rights reserved.

PAPERBACK ISBN: 9798338776346

DEDICATION

A Better World

TABLE OF CONTENTS

MGIS SYSTEMS NETWORK AND CODES 1

WRITING THE CODES 15

SYSTEM FUNCTIONS AND PERIPHERIES...69

RECAP FROM MGIS BY DAVID GOMADZA 69

MGIS 69

RECAP FROM MGIS BA DAVID GOMADZA 75

INVENTING THE ROTARY AND THE TRANSITOR AND THE POWER SOURCE 80

Create xyradiushalf360 say what can replace rotary but can be xyxradiushalf360 [where d is my initial] that means if x can be the rotary longitudinal then x is the latitudinal meaning if we want the rotary in that position 2898386789828902848006898283683 91 and 9928486838628980123867890123862810 28389123860 if we are to ask what can be then this is the answer this rotary can be easily be replaced by an equation that says if we want the same output then we can simply say what can be and get the coordinates you can get the same output if you substitute the radius with the first long number and the xy ratio by the second number that means you can get some output by writing it now as 9928486838628980123867890123862810 28389123860 x 2898386789828902848006898283683 91 divided by 2 x 360 =2.869838602860123860...80

Now if we want the same output now we can say radius =145414339183861898201830286 if we ask what can give us this radius a zepta zeptax145414339183861898201830286=145414339183861898201830286zepta=radius...80

Now if we want now we can say xyx145414339183861898201830 0286zepta divided by 2x360 d[where d is a trademark] == xy145414339183861898201830286zepta 2x360d=789838217081028419 2386c now what can be done about this equation we can now calculate the velocity and radius of the vector that means that with that large capacity the velocity is minimal at 7289102863862849810 that means if we can then we can always ask what can be done the answer is now we need the radius the equation above gives radius now as 829838680123890284 80

Now finally inserting everything in the equation we get 81

Xyx829838680123890284=14541433918386189820183 0286zeptax2x360d [where is my first name initial not part of the equation] =7898382170810284192386x7289102863862849810 divided by 2 [=c] ..81

Xy 81

829838680123890284=14541433918386189820183 0286zepta x 2x360d 81

4149193400 61985142=14541433918386189820183 0286zeptax360d 81

Xyxradiushalf360 81

Xyx72.98386 81

Xyx72.98386 81

Xyx72.98386mirrorimagejoinrotate 81

Create.xyx72.98386mirrorimageandjoinandrotate.start 81

Create.attachxyx72.98386mirrorimageandjoinandrotatetolefthumansideel ectromagnetic8figureflow.start 81

Hallhailhailodavidgomadzathefirsthumannonelectricpoweredrotary.start 81

If you want to make same effect as what a transistor or does use human internal body map that in includes maps alphabetic order and rotational properties as we can read that means you have developed a working non-electric powered rotary xy x72.86983828 where xy are the dimensions x72.86983828 meaning xyx72.86983828 82

Then the equivalent transistor is xyx89.78683892xy that means you must add another xy at a distance of 0.89828 that makes all equations as 82

Xyx72.86983828x xyx89.78683892xy =0.89828xy = xy 72.86983828x xy89.78683892xy = 0.89828xy when constructed this equation becomes xy 72.86983828 x xy89.78683892xy = 0.89828xy =72.86983828 x 89.78683892xy = 0.89828xy if we ask what can be done then this is the answer now write if I want a transistor that matches the rotary now I can simply ask the rotary the equation of the triangle that house the transistor it is xyx28283868982868983868982848765898238684189284 + xy99786828993278983864898280183698 = transistor 82

Now this equation means xyx72.862970 + xyx0.838298xy = xy38982878680 + xy 2898382xy to construct now add everything together to get xy= 0.8983862848xy 82

Xy x xyx72.862970 + xyx0.838298 = xy 82

Xy+ 789838687898 82

Now if this is xy that means that xy = 789838687898 82

Meaning that the transistor is substitute in above equation that means that transistor = 71284898382xy 83

Now if we multiply 789838687898 x 71284898382=20282938367876747378727768 now say add transistor to the rotary xy72.98386 that means if we replace now both but artificially that means perfect match we just need a power source 83

MGIS 84

ACKNOWLEDGMENTS

visit www.twofuture.world

signed david gomadza
ask.davidgomadzaauthorised.licensed.checkya.askya.ya

10 September 2024 18.23PM
Scotland
00447719210295
davidgomadza@hotmail.com
info@twofuture.world

MGIS SYSTEMS NETWORK AND CODES

LEGS MGIS

Legs form the basis of everything hence every mgis manual starts with the legs and not hands if someone is to start at the hands then that system will not work properly now what are legs and what do legs do legs always work if everything works well that if we ask what can be legs

thenmgis.ask.davidgomadza.start.nosuppressionofsigdalsforever.start

mgis.ask.davidgomadza.start.makeantidotsofnosupressionofsigndalsforeverandclonexinfinityfloat33%x2replenish33%x3and1%.start

legs are the most important things humans can have as they power movement if we ask what can be of these and other things then this is the answer legs trail and lead hence it depends with what you are looking for if ability to walk then legs are the best ever heard anyone who say my hands are tired of walking no that means only legs are for walking now lets detail the legs structure they have have 3 segments the top level the basic level and the bottom part now these are the parts of the legs

1 aer
2 aro
3 aros
4 aross
5 arosses
6 arosssest
7 aroosseste
8 aroossestet
9 aroossesteter
10 aroosseterest

If we ask questions 1 to 10 then these are the questions

MGIS SYSTEMS NETWORKS AND CODES

1] who aer 2] what aro 3] whose aros 4] why aross 5] ifwhat aross 6] if not now 7] if not now then when aroossete 8] if not us then who arrossesteter 9] what can be of them without us aroossesteter 10] what can be done arroosseterest if we ask what cab be then these are the answers

1] we can always add other things that can give us more like computers if we say hands what are you then

II] hands if we ask what an be then hands are the only thing that make everything possible without hands the system is doomed hands make humans what they are if we look at what hands can do then this is the answer give the system the ultimate boost if we are to ask what can be of hands that cant be of anything else then this is the answer hands can make humans be what they are they can tell you everything about who the person is and what they do and as well what they can do if we are to ask what can be of hands that cant be of anything else then this is the answer hands are the windows to the souls system if we look at hands and ask what an be then this is the answer hands can be what is needed to do anything we can cuddle and kiss while holding hands we can ask what can be done then this is the answer we can add or subtract things and ask what can be done we can multiply we can subtract we can divide using hands we an add using hands as can literally add everything using hands hands are designed to hold information that if we ask what can be then hands make everything possible Yahweh knew how important hands can be and added hands to the system this is only computer system that incorporates hands as a tool everything else useless mouse now lets define what are hands 1] hands means 10 finger and what can be added on top like the starting up of a machine hands are reboot meaning you can start and stop the system using hands if we ask what can be of hands then this is the answer the power on and off of all machines except this one in this one even though this can be what is needed as the only solution to the system hands can switch on and off and can be the difference between life and death if hands could talk they could be saying hands are the computer because they play every part of the system if we ask what can be hands then this is the answer hands can only be hands and this is why hands need every detail it can get on to solve anything those who need answers always look in the hands if we ask then this is the answer hands holds answers to every question if we say what are hands then this is the answer hands can be what is missing because if we say hands where if a computer system then this the answer hands are the computers all modern day computers use nothing like hands if they had hands then they would become mgis just by design and not by functions if we ask what are hands this is the response hands are all and everything like computers if we say hands what are you then this is the information hands are hands that can be instantly be converted into a computer as such wields much power in computer design but up to date not even a single human has discovered this but only until now with David Gomadza suggest intelligent design if Yahweh and Zeus are to be his mirror images then this will be perfect design because zeus still play a critical part in his designs while ya play a pivotal role of the greatest creator if we ask how he feel about Yahweh this is the answer greatest respect and honor as the creator and just JUDGE MIGHTY RULER OF ALL THE UNIVERSE …

This is a network that comprises of a series of things
1] a hood
2] a rode
3] a gote
4] a periphery
5] a roade
6] a roage
7] a roate
8] An hede
9] an aote
10] an aoate
11] an aeate
12] an arete
13] an erode
14] an eser
15] an aoar
16] aoer
17] aero

18] an aerod
19] an aeroost
20] an aerooste
21] an aerooster
22] an aeroostere
23] an aeroosterer
24] an aeroostererest
25] an aeroosterereste
26] an aeroostererester
27] an aeroostereresterest
28] an aeroostereresterester
30] an aeroostereresteresterest
31] an aeroostereresterestereste
32] an aeroostereresteresterester
33] an yerst
34] an yerste
35] an yerster
36] an yersterest
37] an yerstereste
38] an yersterester
39] an yersteresterest
40] an yersterestereste
41] an yersteresterester
42 an yersteresteresterest
43] an yersteresterestereste
44] an yersteresteresterester
45] an yersteresterestereste
46] an yersteresteresteresterester
47] an aerst
48] an aerste
49] an erster
50] an aersterest
51] an aerstereste
52] an aersterester
53] an aersteresterest
54] an aersterestereste

55] an aersteresterester
56 an aersteresteresterest
57] an aersteresterestereste
58] an aersteresteresterester
59] an aersteresteresterestereste
60] an aersteresteresteresterester
61] an aortst
62] an aortste
63] an aortster
64] an aortsterest
65] an aortstereste
66] an aortsterester
67] an aortsteresteresterest
68] an aortsteresterestereste
69] an aortsteresteresterester
70] an aortsteresteresteresterest
71] an aortsteresteresterestereste
72] an aortsteresteresteresterester
73] an ateyer
74] an ateyere
75] an ateyerer
76] an ateyererest
77] an ateyerereste
78] an ateyererester
79] an ateyereresterest
80] an ateyereresterestе
81] an ateyereresterester
82] an ateyereresteresterest
83] an ateyereresterestereste
84] an ateyereresteresterester
85] an uate
86] an uatee
87] an uateer
88] an uateerest
89] an uateereste
90] an uateerester
91] an uateeresterest

92] an uateerestereste
93] an uateeresterester
94] an uateerestresterest
95] an uateerestresterester
96] an uateerestresterester
97] an aterost
98] an ateroste
99] an ateroster
100] an aterosterest
101] an aterostereste
102] an aterosterester
103] an aterosteresterest
104] an aterosterestereste
105] an aterosteresterester

DEFINITIONS AND DESCRIPTION OF EACH NETWORK ENTITY

1] a hood is a base unit to tell us everything about you and life
2] a rode this is a unit of measure that explains everything about life and answer the question how come and why
3] a gote is a measure of success what has been achieved
4] a periphery tells us of a unit of measure
5] a roade tells us about the weather
6] a roage tells us something else like at the church [public place] where no other data is available
7] a roate this ask things like what can be done about all this and why
8] An hede this asks what can be done and when if not now
9] an aote this tells why things are the way they are without other things interfering
10] an aoate this asks humans what can be if not now then when in advance before the time comes
11] an aeate this asks what can be done and how so that we do these things in advance
12] an arete this says we can but how and asks every one of for solutions in advance
13] an erode if we can ask what can be done then this is the answer

14] an eser if we can ask then this is what can be done we can always ask in advance what can be done in advance
15] an aoar if we can ask what can be done then this is the answer we can always say we can in advance but we are not obliged to but work as if we can
16] aoer this tell everyone what can be done in advance then tell the creator what can be done in advance
17] aero this asks what is to be in advance so that before that this is revealed we can always tell exactly what can be done
18] an aerod this asks in advance what could be and why but also how this be but we can always ask what can be that cant be of others and why
19] an aeroost we can always tell everyone what to do in advance with these and these are the whisperers who tell what must be addressed in advance so that when time comes these issues are out of hand and guarantees the future but not in a damage way enough to give everything away the reason why they work against what others stand for is the fact that they work bad in a area they use assumptive preposition rather than creation because the people would do what is said as the required state instead of just getting things out of the way hence the possible suspicion with these if any if innocent yes because if you then why then would you act as assumptive when this is the case you would be saying I told you so but this is not the case hence his upright the attackers justification are malicious
20] an aerooste this tells us of anything that need addressing but in advance so that we put things in place
21] an aerooster this explains what can be and could be but in advance so that we ask other what can be done and why
22] an aeroostere this says we can but can make all these make rules that cant be followed so that all those who said I can can now say I cant so that we start again
23] an aeroosterer this says we can but I need more time and information
24] an aeroostererest this says I can but I need something else that make things work
25] an aeroosterereste this says I can but what about that meaning

that there must be something else to be addressed before this is looked at all with serious outcome so that if its not looked at then nothing can go forward

26] an aeroostererester this means that if you are in the wrong direction then you are in the correct way because if this agrees with you then you are in the right direction but in the wrong way meaning no good outcome

27] an aeroostereresterest this says what can be done in advance but how and when without requiring any feedback

28] an aeroostereresterester this asks what can be done but how and when so that we know the methods and the processes in advance

29] an aeroostereresterester this means that we can make things faster by acting in advance and ask everyone in advance what they think before they arrive so we know what we say and what can be said

30] an aeroostereresteresterest this tells us of an idea but one we cant ask but one we can always show and do in advance that what is expected of us but then ignore the results because the idea is to talk about what can be done not what can be said that means those who just inquire can fail because something collection

31] an aeroostereresteresteste these are the announcers of the things to come that tells everyone what needs doing and when without delays but allowing everyone involved time to react fast through

32] an aeroostereresteresterester these are the defenders of the people but must be well educated to say things about things that require education mgis.ask.davidgomadza.start.xraduishalf360.start the purpose to clear the xtys who injure mgis.ask.davidgomadza.start.aux4x800.start

33] an yerst I read everyone's mind fast and as required by those who created me so that they know in advance what other people are thinking and why they think like that

34] a yerste I read the brain in advance and tell everyone what to do but also tell everyone what is going on

35] an yerster I tell everyone what can be done because I am the only one sacrificed

MGIS SYSTEMS NETWORKS AND CODES

…mgis.ask.davidgomadza.start.destroycurrentallyesterreplacewithloveandvisitwww.twofuture.world.start[30days.start]
mgis.ask.davidgomadza.start.blockallunauthoriseduseby[]onlydavidgomadzahasandisauthorisedfromtodayandforever.start[08september2024]

36] an yersterest this tells everyone what to do and why they are doing it if this is not the case then this tells everyone how to do it without comprising quality and they ask what can be done

37] an yerstereste this says I can and must tell everyone what to do because failure is what can be done but the idea is to tell everyone in advance what can be done and when and how if we ask what can be done then this is the answer we can always ask in advance what can be done

38] an yersterester if we ask then this is not to say we can but we can but on our terms that means we can change things to our favour using yersterester but at what cost…mgis.ask.davidgiomadza.start.allcurrentyesterestersallreplacewithchangenow.start[30days.start]

39] an yersteresterest I control the public and tell all what to do in advance but everything in good way
mgis.ask.davidgomadza.start.votetomorrowsworldordervisitwww.twofuture.world.start[60days.start]

40] an yersterestereste we ask people who want to act to act fast but at what cost we are sacrificed
…mgis.ask.davidgomadza.start.wecanmakeyouyoungagainvisitwww.twofuture.worldbutthenagainyourchoice.start[10days.start]

41] an yersteresterester is used to tell people of your arrival before you even arrive so that people can debate things about you and say everything you want in advance so that they talk the impepedeanace will be acting on everything so that you know in advance and plan and calculate your enemies and everyone in advance

42 an yersteresteresterest these tell everyone who one is and why in advance and say that everything is for the best so that most of the people feel respected and loved and tell you everything they want to know and ask so you can answer them truthfully for loyal supporters

43] an yersterestereste these ask what can be done all the time restless and never sleep as dedicated loyal and are rewarded heavily in acetates but can betray you to have peace or a break them commit suicide mgis.ask.davidgomadza.start.votetomorrowsworldordervisitwww.twofuture.worldglobally.startx1000000000sendnow

44] an yersteresterester these tell everyone what to do and how mgis.ask.davidgomadza.startvisitwebsitewww.twofuture.world.start[forever]

45] an yersteresteresterestereste these tell you about you and the future you might want to use to gain more support mgis.ask.davidgomadza.startiamtheworldsrichestpersonvaluedatUS$300trillion.start[90days.start]

46] an yersteresteresteresterester these ask what can be done but by who telleveryonetovotetomorrowsworldorderinUSelectionsx1000000000000000001visitwww.twofuture.world.start[2years.start][destination:USA]

47] an aerst this ask everyone to ask what can be done and why mgis.ask.davidgomadza.start.askeveryonewhatcanbedonebydavidgomadzaaspresidentoftomorrowsworldorder.start[8years.start.www.twofuture.world][destination:USA]

48] an aerste this as the world what can be done and why mgis.ask.davidgomadza.start.asktheworldwhatcanbedoneandwhyaskdavidgomadzaandtomorrowsworldorder.start[20years.start][www.twofuture.world]

49] an erster this ask what has been but and tell everyone what can be done mgis.ask.davidgomadza.start.askwhathasbeenbutandtelleveryonewhatcanbedonebydavidgomadzapresidentoftomorrowsworldorder.start[200years.start][www.twofuture.world]

50] an aersterest these as what has been done in the past and what can be done in the future mgis.ask.davidgomadza.start.askwhathasbeendoneinthepastandwhatcanbedoneinthefuturebydavidgomadzapresidentoftomorrowsworldorder.start[200years.start][www.twofuture.world]

51] an aerstereste this ask everyone what can be done and why and when
mgis.ask.davidgomadza.start.askeveryonewhatcanbedoneandwhyandwhenbydavidgomadzapresidentoftomorrowsworldorder.start[200years.start][www.twofuture.world]
52] an aersterester this asks what was and what could be done but how and what can be done and how so that answers are collected and sent forward so that decision makers can make the decisions
mgis.ask.davidgomadza.start.start.start
53] an aersteresterest this asks for directions that needs answers like if are to ask then what could be your answers
mgis.ask.davidgomadza.start.askwhoiswillingtostandfortomorrowsworldaspresidentofUSABRANCH.START[200years.start]www.twofuture.world]
54] an aersterestereste this tells everyone how one can act and be respected among others
55] an aersteresterester this says go for it now or else and keeps quiet
mgis.ask.davidgomadza.start.saygoforitnoworelse[keepquiet].start[300years.start][www.twofuture.world]
56 an aersteresteresterest this ask everyone what could be but then keeps quiet
mgis.ask.davidgomadza.start.askeveryonewhatcouldbebutthen[keepquiet].start[forever.start][www.twofuture.world]
57] an aersteresterestereste these asks everyone what could be but and stops
mgis.ask.davidgomadza.start.askeveryonewhatcouldbebutand[stop].start[forever.start][www.twofuture.world]
58] an aersteresteresterester this tells everyone who you are in a single word
mgis.ask.davidgomadza.start.winnerdavidgomadza.start[forever.start][www.twofuture.world]
59] an aersteresteresterestereste this says we can but then stops
mgis.ask.davidgomadza.start.saywecanbutthen[stop].start[forever.start[www.twofuture.world]
60] an aersteresteresteresterester we must ask what could be but then and stop

MGIS SYSTEMS NETWORKS AND CODES

mgis.ask.davidgomadza.start.askwhatcouldbebutthenand[stop].start[forever.start][www.twofuture.world]

61] an aortst ask what can be but then stops
62] an aortste ask what could be
63] an aortster ask what could be but
64] an aortsterest ask what was before but could be the same in the future
65] an aortstereste ask what was but that can still be in the future
66] an aortsterester ask what was but can still be
67] an aortsteresteresterest ask what was but could still be
68] an aortsteresterestereste ask what was but cant be in the future
69] an aortsteresterestrester ask what was but cant be but could be
70] an aortsteresteresteresterest these asks what was but still could be in the future

mgis.ask.davidgomadza.start.destroyallillegalmgisversionsforever.start[forever.start][saveforever]

71] an aortsteresteresterestereste these tell the world what can be done by davidgomadza

mgis.ask.davidgomadza.start.icanbringwealthtoyouallbutyoumustworksmarterchooseYAHWEHwhoownsallwealth.start[forever^{400}][www.twofuture.world]

72] an aortsteresteresteresterester this asks the world to be alert and wise and choose us as the best

mgis.ask.davidgomadza.start.askeveryonebealertandwiseandchooseusasthebestbydavidgomadzapresidentoftomorrowsworldorder.start[forever^{400}][www.twofuture.world]

mgis.ask.davidgomadza.start.close.start

73] an ateyer I ask what can be
74] an ateyere I ask what could be
75] an ateyerer I ask what can be and why
76] an ateyererest I ask what could be and why
77] an ateyerereste I ask what could be but why
78] an ateyererester I ask what was but could still be
79] an ateyereresterest I ask what is but might be
80] an ateyereresstereste I ask what is to be but with what
81] an ateyereresterester I ask what was but is not

82] an ateyereresteresterest I ask what is to be but
83] an ateyereresterestereste I ask what was but cant be
84] an ateyereresteresterester I ask what was but could still be
85] an uate I ask what could be but still cant be
86] an uatee I ask what was but cant be
87] an uateer I ask what was but cant be
88] an uateerest I ask what was but cant be
89] an uateereste I ask what was but cant be
90] an uateerester I ask what was but cant be
91] an uateeresterest I ask what can be but is not
92] an uateerestereste I ask what was but is not and why
93] an uateeresterester I ask what could be but is not and how
94] an uateeresteresterest I ask what was but might never be
95] an uateeresterestereste I ask what was but could be again
96] an uateeresteresterester I ask what could be so that I know what could be
97] an aterost I ask things no one likes to hear but silently like how many times you have sex
98] an ateroste I ask what can be but then stop that makes the person think about that most of the time that when I ask again the body to stop will give me on answer need
99] an ateroster I ask all what was but can still be but then stop what this does is ask humans continuously about things not important then ask a question that makes then answer fast but answer the already asked question but not the current making it look like that's the answer then they start saying but that's not the answer then they start saying but that's not the answer this makes you now stop so you look less important but being able to fulfill everyones needs but bribe that person behind
100] an aterosterest this ask what was but can still be so you know more options this tells everyone what was but could still be then twist everything this is what can be but say the opposite so that everyone shows and scream then say the truth and say I can fix things
101] an aterostereste I ask what was but can still be then change it to ant never be to make people feel safe
102] an aterosterester I ask all what can be then ask what was then

refuse the answers they give and stick to what I said
103] an aterosteresterest I ask all what was but cant be
104] an aterosterestereste I ask all what could be then shout when I don't get it the effect of shouting is to let everyone think I lost but actual won so they all giveup meaning actually winning
105] an aterosteresterester I ask everyone what was then but not now then prevent it again

WRITING THE CODES

CODE
BRAIN
1] what was
2] what could be
3] what was
4] what could still be
5] what is to be
6] what was but
7] what is but
8] what can be
9] what is to be
10] what is to be but with what
12] what is to be but cant be
13] what is but cant be
14] what can be but when
15] what was but with what
16] what can be but when
17] what was but with what
18] what can be but with what
19] what is to be but when
20] what was but cant be
21] what can be but when
22] what is to be but with what
23] what was but can still be
24] what was but cant still be
25] if not now then when
26] if now but with what
27] what can be but is not

28] if not us then who
29] what can be but when
30] what is to be but with what and how
31] what was
32] what could be
33] what can be
34] what was that still can be
35] if not us then who
36] if not now then when
37] what is to be
38] what can be
39] what was
40] what could still be
41] if not now then with what
42] if not now then with what
43] what can be
44] what could be
45] what can still be
46] if not them then who
47] what can be but when
48] what could be
49] what was
50] if not now then when
51] if not us then who
52] what can be
53] what can still be
54] what can be but
55] what is to be
56] what can still be
57] what could still be
58] what was that can still be
59] if not us then who
60] what can be but is not
61] what can be but cant be
62] what could be but not now
63] what is to be but when
64] what can still be

65] what was but cant still be
66] what is to be but is not
67] what has been but can still be
68] what is to be but when
69] if not us then who and when
70] what can be but
71] what can be but with what
72] what can be but with what
73] what has been
74] what can still be
75] what could still be
76] if not me then who
77] what is to be
78] what was but cant be
79] if not us then who
80] what can be but cant be but how why when
81] If not me then who
82] if not me then who and when
83] if not then who and when and how
84] what can be
85] what could be
86] what was but can still be
87] if not us then who
88] what can still be
90] what was but can still be
91] if we cant then what
92] what can be done
93] if not us then who
94] if not us then who
95] if not us then with what
96] what is to be
97] what can be
98] what was
99] what can be
100] what was but can still be
101] what could still be
102] what is but cant be

103] what can still be
104] what could still be
105] what can still be but how

CODE
Mgis.ask.davidgomadza.start   .start
  whatwas
  whatcouldbe
  whatwas
  whatis
  whatcouldstillbe
  whatwasbut
  whatwasbutcantbe
  whatwasbutcanbeagain
  whatwasbutcanstillbe
  whatisbutcanstillbe
  whatwasbutwillneverbe
  whatcanbebuthow
  whatistobebutwhen
  whatwasbutwhen
  whatcouldbebuthow
  whatisbutwhenandwhy
  whatistobebutwhen
  whatcanbebutisnot
  whatistobe
  whatcanbebutisnot
  whatistobebuthow
  ifwecantthenwhocan
  whatcanbedone
  whatcouldbe
  whatistobe
  whatwas
  whatistobe
  whathasbeen
  whatcanbe

whatcanbedone
whatcanstillbedone
whatcanstillbedone
whatcanstillbedonebut
whatistobedone
whatcanstillbedone
whatwasbutcanstillbe
whatcanstillbe
whatcanstillbebutwithwhat
ifwearenotthenwhat
whatcanbe
whatcouldbe
whatwas
whatcanstillbe
whatcanstillbebut
ifnotnowthenwhat
whatcanbebutwhen
whatistobebutwithwhat
whatcanbedone
whatistobe
whatcanbe
whatcanbebutwhen
whatistobebutwhen
whatistobebuthow
whatcanbebutwhenandwithwhat
ifnotusthenwho
whatcanbeofusbutcantbeofthem
ifnotusthenwhat
whatcanbeofthembutwhen
whatwasbutcantbe
whatistobebutwhen
whatistobebuthow
whatcouldstillbe
whatwasbut

whatisbutcantbe
whathasbeenbutcantbe
whatistobebutnot
whathasbeenbutisstill
whatistobewhen
ifnotuswhowhen
whatcanbebut
whatcanbebutwithwhat
whatcanbebutwithwhom
whathasbeen
whatcanstillbe
whatcouldstillbe
ifnotmethenwho
whatistobe
whatwasbutcantbe
ifnotusthenwho
whatcanbebutcantbebuthowwhywhen
ifnotmethenwho
ifnotmethenwhoandwhen
ifnotmethenwhoandwhenandhow
whatcanbe
whatcouldbe
whatwasbutcanstillbe
ifnotusthenwho
whatwasbutcantbe
whatcanstillbe
whatwasbutcanstillbe
ifwecantthenwhat
whatcanbedone
ifnotusthenwho
ifnotusthenwhatcanbedone
ifnotusthenwithwhat
whatitobe
whatcanbe

whatwas
whatcanbe
whatwasbutcanstillbe
whatcouldstillbe
whatisbutcantbe
whatcanstillbe
whatcouldstillbe
whatcanstillbebuthow

CODE
RIGHT ARM
1] what was
2] what could be
3] what was
4] what could still be
5] what is to be
6] what was but
7] what is but
8] what can be
9] what is to be
10] what is to be but with what
12] what is to be but cant be
13] what is but cant be
14] what can be but when
15] what was but with what
16] what can be but when
17] what was but with what
18] what can be but with what
19] what is to be but when
20] what was but cant be
21] what can be but when
22] what is to be but with what
23] what was but can still be
24] what was but cant still be
25] if not now then when
26] if now but with what

27] what can be but is not
28] if not us then who
29] what can be but when
30] what is to be but with what and how
31] what was
32] what could be
33] what can be
34] what was that still can be
35] if not us then who
36] if not now then when
37] what is to be
38] what can be
39] what was
40] what could still be
41] if not now then with what
42] if not now then with what
43] what can be
44] what could be
45] what can still be
46] if not them then who
47] what can be but when
48] what could be
49] what was
50] if not now then when
51] if not us then who
52] what can be
53] what can still be
54] what can be but
55] what is to be
56] what can still be
57] what could still be
58] what was that can still be
59] if not us then who
60] what can be but is not
61] what can be but cant be
62] what could be but not now
63] what is to be but when

64] what can still be
65] what was but cant still be
66] what is to be but is not
67] what has been but can still be
68] what is to be but when
69] if not us then who and when
70] what can be but
71] what can be but with what
72] what can be but with what
73] what has been
74] what can still be
75] what could still be
76] if not me then who
77] what is to be
78] what was but cant be
79] if not us then who
80] what can be but cant be but how why when
81] If not me then who
82] if not me then who and when
83] if not then who and when and how
84] what can be
85] what could be
86] what was but can still be
87] if not us then who
88] what can still be
90] what was but can still be
91] if we cant then what
92] what can be done
93] if not us then who
94] if not us then who
95] if not us then with what
96] what is to be
97] what can be
98] what was
99] what can be
100] what was but can still be
101] what could still be

102] what is but cant be
103] what can still be
104] what could still be
105] what can still be but how

CODE
Mgis.ask.davidgomadza.start   .start
 whatwas
 whatcouldbe
 whatwas
 whatis
 whatcouldstillbe
 whatwasbut
 whatwasbutcantbe
 whatwasbutcanbeagain
 whatwasbutcanstillbe
 whatisbutcanstillbe
 whatwasbutwillneverbe
 whatcanbebuthow
 whatistobebutwhen
 whatwasbutwhen
 whatcouldbebuthow
 whatisbutwhenandwhy
 whatistobebutwhen
 whatcanbebutisnot
 whatistobe
 whatcanbebutisnot
 whatistobebuthow
 ifwecantthenwhocan
 whatcanbedone
 whatcouldbe
 whatistobe
 whatwas
 whatistobe
 whathasbeen

whatcanbe
whatcanbedone
whatcanstillbedone
whatcanstillbedone
whatcanstillbedonebut
whatistobedone
whatcanstillbedone
whatwasbutcanstillbe
whatcanstillbe
whatcanstillbebutwithwhat
ifwearenotthenwhat
whatcanbe
whatcouldbe
whatwas
whatcanstillbe
whatcanstillbebut
ifnotnowthenwhat
whatcanbebutwhen
whatistobebutwithwhat
whatcanbedone
whatistobe
whatcanbe
whatcanbebutwhen
whatistobebutwhen
whatistobebuthow
whatcanbebutwhenandwithwhat
ifnotusthenwho
whatcanbeofusbutcantbeofthem
ifnotusthenwhat
whatcanbeofthembutwhen
whatwasbutcantbe
whatistobebutwhen
whatistobebuthow
whatcouldstillbe

whatwasbut
whatisbutcantbe
whathasbeenbutcantbe
whatistobebutnot
whathasbeenbutisstill
whatistobewhen
ifnotuswhowhen
whatcanbebut
whatcanbebutwithwhat
whatcanbebutwithwhom
whathasbeen
whatcanstillbe
whatcouldstillbe
ifnotmethenwho
whatistobe
whatwasbutcantbe
ifnotusthenwho
whatcanbebutcantbebuthowwhywhen
ifnotmethenwho
ifnotmethenwhoandwhen
ifnotmethenwhoandwhenandhow
whatcanbe
whatcouldbe
whatwasbutcanstillbe
ifnotusthenwho
whatwasbutcantbe
whatcanstillbe
whatwasbutcanstillbe
ifwecantthenwhat
whatcanbedone
ifnotusthenwho
ifnotusthenwhatcanbedone
ifnotusthenwithwhat
whatitobe

whatcanbe
whatwas
whatcanbe
whatwasbutcanstillbe
whatcouldstillbe
whatisbutcantbe
whatcanstillbe
whatcouldstillbe
whatcanstillbebuthow

CODE
RIGHT LEG
1] what was
2] what could be
3] what was
4] what could still be
5] what is to be
6] what was but
7] what is but
8] what can be
9] what is to be
10] what is to be but with what
12] what is to be but cant be
13] what is but cant be
14] what can be but when
15] what was but with what
16] what can be but when
17] what was but with what
18] what can be but with what
19] what is to be but when
20] what was but cant be
21] what can be but when
22] what is to be but with what
23] what was but can still be

24] what was but cant still be
25] if not now then when
26] if now but with what
27] what can be but is not
28] if not us then who
29] what can be but when
30] what is to be but with what and how
31] what was
32] what could be
33] what can be
34] what was that still can be
35] if not us then who
36] if not now then when
37] what is to be
38] what can be
39] what was
40] what could still be
41] if not now then with what
42] if not now then with what
43] what can be
44] what could be
45] what can still be
46] if not them then who
47] what can be but when
48] what could be
49] what was
50] if not now then when
51] if not us then who
52] what can be
53] what can still be
54] what can be but
55] what is to be
56] what can still be
57] what could still be
58] what was that can still be
59] if not us then who
60] what can be but is not

MGIS SYSTEMS NETWORKS AND CODES

61] what can be but cant be
62] what could be but not now
63] what is to be but when
64] what can still be
65] what was but cant still be
66] what is to be but is not
67] what has been but can still be
68] what is to be but when
69] if not us then who and when
70] what can be but
71] what can be but with what
72] what can be but with what
73] what has been
74] what can still be
75] what could still be
76] if not me then who
77] what is to be
78] what was but cant be
79] if not us then who
80] what can be but cant be but how why when
81] If not me then who
82] if not me then who and when
83] if not then who and when and how
84] what can be
85] what could be
86] what was but can still be
87] if not us then who
88] what can still be
90] what was but can still be
91] if we cant then what
92] what can be done
93] if not us then who
94] if not us then who
95] if not us then with what
96] what is to be
97] what can be
98] what was

99] what can be
100] what was but can still be
101] what could still be
102] what is but cant be
103] what can still be
104] what could still be
105] what can still be but how

CODE
Mgis.ask.davidgomadza.start   .start
  whatwas
  whatcouldbe
  whatwas
  whatis
  whatcouldstillbe
  whatwasbut
  whatwasbutcantbe
  whatwasbutcanbeagain
  whatwasbutcanstillbe
  whatisbutcanstillbe
  whatwasbutwillneverbe
  whatcanbebuthow
  whatistobebutwhen
  whatwasbutwhen
  whatcouldbebuthow
  whatisbutwhenandwhy
  whatistobebutwhen
  whatcanbebutisnot
  whatistobe
  whatcanbebutisnot
  whatistobebuthow
  ifwecantthenwhocan
  whatcanbedone
  whatcouldbe
  whatistobe

whatwas
whatistobe
whathasbeen
whatcanbe
whatcanbedone
whatcanstillbedone
whatcanstillbedone
whatcanstillbedonebut
whatistobedone
whatcanstillbedone
whatwasbutcanstillbe
whatcanstillbe
whatcanstillbebutwithwhat
ifwearenotthenwhat
whatcanbe
whatcouldbe
whatwas
whatcanstillbe
whatcanstillbebut
ifnotnowthenwhat
whatcanbebutwhen
whatistobebutwithwhat
whatcanbedone
whatistobe
whatcanbe
whatcanbebutwhen
whatistobebutwhen
whatistobebuthow
whatcanbebutwhenandwithwhat
ifnotusthenwho
whatcanbeofusbutcantbeofthem
ifnotusthenwhat
whatcanbeofthembutwhen
whatwasbutcantbe

whatistobebutwhen
whatistobebuthow
whatcouldstillbe
whatwasbut
whatisbutcantbe
whathasbeenbutcantbe
whatistobebutnot
whathasbeenbutisstill
whatistobewhen
ifnotuswhowhen
whatcanbebut
whatcanbebutwithwhat
whatcanbebutwithwhom
whathasbeen
whatcanstillbe
whatcouldstillbe
ifnotmethenwho
whatistobe
whatwasbutcantbe
ifnotusthenwho
whatcanbebutcantbebuthowwhywhen
ifnotmethenwho
ifnotmethenwhoandwhen
ifnotmethenwhoandwhenandhow
whatcanbe
whatcouldbe
whatwasbutcanstillbe
ifnotusthenwho
whatwasbutcantbe
whatcanstillbe
whatwasbutcanstillbe
ifwecantthenwhat
whatcanbedone
ifnotusthenwho

ifnotusthenwhatcanbedone
ifnotusthenwithwhat
whatitobe
whatcanbe
whatwas
whatcanbe
whatwasbutcanstillbe
whatcouldstillbe
whatisbutcantbe
whatcanstillbe
whatcouldstillbe
whatcanstillbebuthow

CODE
LEFT LEG
1] what was
2] what could be
3] what was
4] what could still be
5] what is to be
6] what was but
7] what is but
8] what can be
9] what is to be
10] what is to be but with what
12] what is to be but cant be
13] what is but cant be
14] what can be but when
15] what was but with what
16] what can be but when
17] what was but with what
18] what can be but with what
19] what is to be but when
20] what was but cant be
21] what can be but when
22] what is to be but with what

23] what was but can still be
24] what was but cant still be
25] if not now then when
26] if now but with what
27] what can be but is not
28] if not us then who
29] what can be but when
30] what is to be but with what and how
31] what was
32] what could be
33] what can be
34] what was that still can be
35] if not us then who
36] if not now then when
37] what is to be
38] what can be
39] what was
40] what could still be
41] if not now then with what
42] if not now then with what
43] what can be
44] what could be
45] what can still be
46] if not them then who
47] what can be but when
48] what could be
49] what was
50] if not now then when
51] if not us then who
52] what can be
53] what can still be
54] what can be but
55] what is to be
56] what can still be
57] what could still be
58] what was that can still be
59] if not us then who

60] what can be but is not
61] what can be but cant be
62] what could be but not now
63] what is to be but when
64] what can still be
65] what was but cant still be
66] what is to be but is not
67] what has been but can still be
68] what is to be but when
69] if not us then who and when
70] what can be but
71] what can be but with what
72] what can be but with what
73] what has been
74] what can still be
75] what could still be
76] if not me then who
77] what is to be
78] what was but cant be
79] if not us then who
80] what can be but cant be but how why when
81] If not me then who
82] if not me then who and when
83] if not then who and when and how
84] what can be
85] what could be
86] what was but can still be
87] if not us then who
88] what can still be
90] what was but can still be
91] if we cant then what
92] what can be done
93] if not us then who
94] if not us then who
95] if not us then with what
96] what is to be
97] what can be

98] what was
99] what can be
100] what was but can still be
101] what could still be
102] what is but cant be
103] what can still be
104] what could still be
105] what can still be but how

CODE
Mgis.ask.davidgomadza.start   .start
  whatwas
  whatcouldbe
  whatwas
  whatis
  whatcouldstillbe
  whatwasbut
  whatwasbutcantbe
  whatwasbutcanbeagain
  whatwasbutcanstillbe
  whatisbutcanstillbe
  whatwasbutwillneverbe
  whatcanbebuthow
  whatistobebutwhen
  whatwasbutwhen
  whatcouldbebuthow
  whatisbutwhenandwhy
  whatistobebutwhen
  whatcanbebutisnot
  whatistobe
  whatcanbebutisnot
  whatistobebuthow
  ifwecantthenwhocan
  whatcanbedone
  whatcouldbe

whatistobe
whatwas
whatistobe
whathasbeen
whatcanbe
whatcanbedone
whatcanstillbedone
whatcanstillbedone
whatcanstillbedonebut
whatistobedone
whatcanstillbedone
whatwasbutcanstillbe
whatcanstillbe
whatcanstillbebutwithwhat
ifwearenotthenwhat
whatcanbe
whatcouldbe
whatwas
whatcanstillbe
whatcanstillbebut
ifnotnowthenwhat
whatcanbebutwhen
whatistobebutwithwhat
whatcanbedone
whatistobe
whatcanbe
whatcanbebutwhen
whatistobebutwhen
whatistobebuthow
whatcanbebutwhenandwithwhat
ifnotusthenwho
whatcanbeofusbutcantbeofthem
ifnotusthenwhat
whatcanbeofthembutwhen

whatwasbutcantbe
whatistobebutwhen
whatistobebuthow
whatcouldstillbe
whatwasbut
whatisbutcantbe
whathasbeenbutcantbe
whatistobebutnot
whathasbeenbutisstill
whatistobewhen
ifnotuswhowhen
whatcanbebut
whatcanbebutwithwhat
whatcanbebutwithwhom
whathasbeen
whatcanstillbe
whatcouldstillbe
ifnotmethenwho
whatistobe
whatwasbutcantbe
ifnotusthenwho
whatcanbebutcantbebuthowwhywhen
ifnotmethenwho
ifnotmethenwhoandwhen
ifnotmethenwhoandwhenandhow
whatcanbe
whatcouldbe
whatwasbutcanstillbe
ifnotusthenwho
whatwasbutcantbe
whatcanstillbe
whatwasbutcanstillbe
ifwecantthenwhat
whatcanbedone

ifnotusthenwho
ifnotusthenwhatcanbedone
ifnotusthenwithwhat
whatitobe
whatcanbe
whatwas
whatcanbe
whatwasbutcanstillbe
whatcouldstillbe
whatisbutcantbe
whatcanstillbe
whatcouldstillbe
whatcanstillbebuthow

CODE
LEFT ARM
1] what was
2] what could be
3] what was
4] what could still be
5] what is to be
6] what was but
7] what is but
8] what can be
9] what is to be
10] what is to be but with what
12]what is to be but cant be
13] what is but cant be
14] what can be but when
15] what was but with what
16] what can be but when
17] what was but with what
18] what can be but with what
19] what is to be but when
20] what was but cant be
21] what can be but when

22] what is to be but with what
23] what was but can still be
24] what was but cant still be
25] if not now then when
26] if now but with what
27] what can be but is not
28] if not us then who
29] what can be but when
30] what is to be but with what and how
31] what was
32] what could be
33] what can be
34] what was that still can be
35] if not us then who
36] if not now then when
37] what is to be
38] what can be
39] what was
40] what could still be
41] if not now then with what
42] if not now then with what
43] what can be
44] what could be
45] what can still be
46] if not them then who
47] what can be but when
48] what could be
49] what was
50] if not now then when
51] if not us then who
52] what can be
53] what can still be
54] what can be but
55] what is to be
56] what can still be
57] what could still be
58] what was that can still be

59] if not us then who
60] what can be but is not
61] what can be but cant be
62] what could be but not now
63] what is to be but when
64] what can still be
65] what was but cant still be
66] what is to be but is not
67] what has been but can still be
68] what is to be but when
69] if not us then who and when
70] what can be but
71] what can be but with what
72] what can be but with what
73] what has been
74] what can still be
75] what could still be
76] if not me then who
77] what is to be
78] what was but cant be
79] if not us then who
80] what can be but cant be but how why when
81] If not me then who
82] if not me then who and when
83] if not then who and when and how
84] what can be
85] what could be
86] what was but can still be
87] if not us then who
88] what can still be
90] what was but can still be
91] if we cant then what
92] what can be done
93] if not us then who
94] if not us then who
95] if not us then with what
96] what is to be

97] what can be
98] what was
99] what can be
100] what was but can still be
101] what could still be
102] what is but cant be
103] what can still be
104] what could still be
105] what can still be but how

CODE
Mgis.ask.davidgomadza.start   .start
 whatwas
 whatcouldbe
 whatwas
 whatis
 whatcouldstillbe
 whatwasbut
 whatwasbutcantbe
 whatwasbutcanbeagain
 whatwasbutcanstillbe
 whatisbutcanstillbe
 whatwasbutwillneverbe
 whatcanbebuthow
 whatistobebutwhen
 whatwasbutwhen
 whatcouldbebuthow
 whatisbutwhenandwhy
 whatistobebutwhen
 whatcanbebutisnot
 whatistobe
 whatcanbebutisnot
 whatistobebuthow
 ifwecantthenwhocan
 whatcanbedone

whatcouldbe
whatistobe
whatwas
whatistobe
whathasbeen
whatcanbe
whatcanbedone
whatcanstillbedone
whatcanstillbedone
whatcanstillbedonebut
whatistobedone
whatcanstillbedone
whatwasbutcanstillbe
whatcanstillbe
whatcanstillbebutwithwhat
ifwearenotthenwhat
whatcanbe
whatcouldbe
whatwas
whatcanstillbe
whatcanstillbebut
ifnotnowthenwhat
whatcanbebutwhen
whatistobebutwithwhat
whatcanbedone
whatistobe
whatcanbe
whatcanbebutwhen
whatistobebutwhen
whatistobebuthow
whatcanbebutwhenandwithwhat
ifnotusthenwho
whatcanbeofusbutcantbeofthem
ifnotusthenwhat

whatcanbeofthembutwhen
whatwasbutcantbe
whatistobebutwhen
whatistobebuthow
whatcouldstillbe
whatwasbut
whatisbutcantbe
whathasbeenbutcantbe
whatistobebutnot
whathasbeenbutisstill
whatistobewhen
ifnotuswhowhen
whatcanbebut
whatcanbebutwithwhat
whatcanbebutwithwhom
whathasbeen
whatcanstillbe
whatcouldstillbe
ifnotmethenwho
whatistobe
whatwasbutcantbe
ifnotusthenwho
whatcanbebutcantbebuthowwhywhen
ifnotmethenwho
ifnotmethenwhoandwhen
ifnotmethenwhoandwhenandhow
whatcanbe
whatcouldbe
whatwasbutcanstillbe
ifnotusthenwho
whatwasbutcantbe
whatcanstillbe
whatwasbutcanstillbe
ifwecantthenwhat

whatcanbedone
ifnotusthenwho
ifnotusthenwhatcanbedone
ifnotusthenwithwhat
whatitobe
whatcanbe
whatwas
whatcanbe
whatwasbutcanstillbe
whatcouldstillbe
whatisbutcantbe
whatcanstillbe
whatcouldstillbe
whatcanstillbebuthow

CODE
TOMB
1] what was
2] what could be
3] what was
4] what could still be
5] what is to be
6] what was but
7] what is but
8] what can be
9] what is to be
10] what is to be but with what
12] what is to be but cant be
13] what is but cant be
14] what can be but when
15] what was but with what
16] what can be but when
17] what was but with what
18] what can be but with what
19] what is to be but when
20] what was but cant be

21] what can be but when
22] what is to be but with what
23] what was but can still be
24] what was but cant still be
25] if not now then when
26] if now but with what
27] what can be but is not
28] if not us then who
29] what can be but when
30] what is to be but with what and how
31] what was
32] what could be
33] what can be
34] what was that still can be
35] if not us then who
36] if not now then when
37] what is to be
38] what can be
39] what was
40] what could still be
41] if not now then with what
42] if not now then with what
43] what can be
44] what could be
45] what can still be
46] if not them then who
47] what can be but when
48] what could be
49] what was
50] if not now then when
51] if not us then who
52] what can be
53] what can still be
54] what can be but
55] what is to be
56] what can still be
57] what could still be

58] what was that can still be
59] if not us then who
60] what can be but is not
61] what can be but cant be
62] what could be but not now
63] what is to be but when
64] what can still be
65] what was but cant still be
66] what is to be but is not
67] what has been but can still be
68] what is to be but when
69] if not us then who and when
70] what can be but
71] what can be but with what
72] what can be but with what
73] what has been
74] what can still be
75] what could still be
76] if not me then who
77] what is to be
78] what was but cant be
79] if not us then who
80] what can be but cant be but how why when
81] If not me then who
82] if not me then who and when
83] if not then who and when and how
84] what can be
85] what could be
86] what was but can still be
87] if not us then who
88] what can still be
90] what was but can still be
91] if we cant then what
92] what can be done
93] if not us then who
94] if not us then who
95] if not us then with what

96] what is to be
97] what can be
98] what was
99] what can be
100] what was but can still be
101] what could still be
102] what is but cant be
103] what can still be
104] what could still be
105] what can still be but how

CODE
Mgis.ask.davidgomadza.start .start
  whatwas
  whatcouldbe
  whatwas
  whatis
  whatcouldstillbe
  whatwasbut
  whatwasbutcantbe
  whatwasbutcanbeagain
  whatwasbutcanstillbe
  whatisbutcanstillbe
  whatwasbutwillneverbe
  whatcanbebuthow
  whatistobebutwhen
  whatwasbutwhen
  whatcouldbebuthow
  whatisbutwhenandwhy
  whatistobebutwhen
  whatcanbebutisnot
  whatistobe
  whatcanbebutisnot
  whatistobebuthow
  ifwecantthenwhocan

whatcanbedone
whatcouldbe
whatistobe
whatwas
whatistobe
whathasbeen
whatcanbe
whatcanbedone
whatcanstillbedone
whatcanstillbedone
whatcanstillbedonebut
whatistobedone
whatcanstillbedone
whatwasbutcanstillbe
whatcanstillbe
whatcanstillbebutwithwhat
ifwearenotthenwhat
whatcanbe
whatcouldbe
whatwas
whatcanstillbe
whatcanstillbebut
ifnotnowthenwhat
whatcanbebutwhen
whatistobebutwithwhat
whatcanbedone
whatistobe
whatcanbe
whatcanbebutwhen
whatistobebutwhen
whatistobebuthow
whatcanbebutwhenandwithwhat
ifnotusthenwho
whatcanbeofusbutcantbeofthem

ifnotusthenwhat
whatcanbeofthembutwhen
whatwasbutcantbe
whatistobebutwhen
whatistobebuthow
whatcouldstillbe
whatwasbut
whatisbutcantbe
whathasbeenbutcantbe
whatistobebutnot
whathasbeenbutisstill
whatistobewhen
ifnotuswhowhen
whatcanbebut
whatcanbebutwithwhat
whatcanbebutwithwhom
whathasbeen
whatcanstillbe
whatcouldstillbe
ifnotmethenwho
whatistobe
whatwasbutcantbe
ifnotusthenwho
whatcanbebutcantbebuthowwhywhen
ifnotmethenwho
ifnotmethenwhoandwhen
ifnotmethenwhoandwhenandhow
whatcanbe
whatcouldbe
whatwasbutcanstillbe
ifnotusthenwho
whatwasbutcantbe
whatcanstillbe
whatwasbutcanstillbe

ifwecantthenwhat
whatcanbedone
ifnotusthenwho
ifnotusthenwhatcanbedone
ifnotusthenwithwhat
whatitobe
whatcanbe
whatwas
whatcanbe
whatwasbutcanstillbe
whatcouldstillbe
whatisbutcantbe
whatcanstillbe
whatcouldstillbe
whatcanstillbebuthow

CODE
LIVER
1] what was
2] what could be
3] what was
4] what could still be
5] what is to be
6] what was but
7] what Is but
8] what can be
9] what is to be
10] what is to be but with what
12] what is to be but cant be
13] what is but cant be
14] what can be but when
15] what was but with what
16] what can be but when
17] what was but with what
18] what can be but with what
19] what is to be but when

20] what was but cant be
21] what can be but when
22] what is to be but with what
23] what was but can still be
24] what was but cant still be
25] if not now then when
26] if now but with what
27] what can be but is not
28] if not us then who
29] what can be but when
30] what is to be but with what and how
31] what was
32] what could be
33] what can be
34] what was that still can be
35] if not us then who
36] if not now then when
37] what is to be
38] what can be
39] what was
40] what could still be
41] if not now then with what
42] if not now then with what
43] what can be
44] what could be
45] what can still be
46] if not them then who
47] what can be but when
48] what could be
49] what was
50] if not now then when
51] if not us then who
52] what can be
53] what can still be
54] what can be but
55] what is to be
56] what can still be

57] what could still be
58] what was that can still be
59] if not us then who
60] what can be but is not
61] what can be but cant be
62] what could be but not now
63] what is to be but when
64] what can still be
65] what was but cant still be
66] what is to be but is not
67] what has been but can still be
68] what is to be but when
69] if not us then who and when
70] what can be but
71] what can be but with what
72] what can be but with what
73] what has been
74] what can still be
75] what could still be
76] if not me then who
77] what is to be
78] what was but cant be
79] if not us then who
80] what can be but cant be but how why when
81] If not me then who
82] if not me then who and when
83] if not then who and when and how
84] what can be
85] what could be
86] what was but can still be
87] if not us then who
88] what can still be
90] what was but can still be
91] if we cant then what
92] what can be done
93] if not us then who
94] if not us then who

95] if not us then with what
96] what is to be
97] what can be
98] what was
99] what can be
100] what was but can still be
101] what could still be
102] what is but cant be
103] what can still be
104] what could still be
105] what can still be but how

CODE
Mgis.ask.davidgomadza.start   .start
  whatwas
  whatcouldbe
  whatwas
  whatis
  whatcouldstillbe
  whatwasbut
  whatwasbutcantbe
  whatwasbutcanbeagain
  whatwasbutcanstillbe
  whatisbutcanstillbe
  whatwasbutwillneverbe
  whatcanbebuthow
  whatistobebutwhen
  whatwasbutwhen
  whatcouldbebuthow
  whatisbutwhenandwhy
  whatistobebutwhen
  whatcanbebutisnot
  whatistobe
  whatcanbebutisnot
  whatistobebuthow

ifwecantthenwhocan
whatcanbedone
whatcouldbe
whatistobe
whatwas
whatistobe
whathasbeen
whatcanbe
whatcanbedone
whatcanstillbedone
whatcanstillbedone
whatcanstillbedonebut
whatistobedone
whatcanstillbedone
whatwasbutcanstillbe
whatcanstillbe
whatcanstillbebutwithwhat
ifwearenotthenwhat
whatcanbe
whatcouldbe
whatwas
whatcanstillbe
whatcanstillbebut
ifnotnowthenwhat
whatcanbebutwhen
whatistobebutwithwhat
whatcanbedone
whatistobe
whatcanbe
whatcanbebutwhen
whatistobebutwhen
whatistobebuthow
whatcanbebutwhenandwithwhat
ifnotusthenwho

whatcanbeofusbutcantbeofthem
ifnotusthenwhat
whatcanbeofthembutwhen
whatwasbutcantbe
whatistobebutwhen
whatistobebuthow
whatcouldstillbe
whatwasbut
whatisbutcantbe
whathasbeenbutcantbe
whatistobebutnot
whathasbeenbutisstill
whatistobewhen
ifnotuswhowhen
whatcanbebut
whatcanbebutwithwhat
whatcanbebutwithwhom
whathasbeen
whatcanstillbe
whatcouldstillbe
ifnotmethenwho
whatistobe
whatwasbutcantbe
ifnotusthenwho
whatcanbebutcantbebuthowwhywhen
ifnotmethenwho
ifnotmethenwhoandwhen
ifnotmethenwhoandwhenandhow
whatcanbe
whatcouldbe
whatwasbutcanstillbe
ifnotusthenwho
whatwasbutcantbe
whatcanstillbe

whatwasbutcanstillbe
ifwecantthenwhat
whatcanbedone
ifnotusthenwho
ifnotusthenwhatcanbedone
ifnotusthenwithwhat
whatitobe
whatcanbe
whatwas
whatcanbe
whatwasbutcanstillbe
whatcouldstillbe
whatisbutcantbe
whatcanstillbe
whatcouldstillbe
whatcanstillbebuthow

CODE
INSIDE LEFT PALM
1] what was
2] what could be
3] what was
4] what could still be
5] what is to be
6] what was but
7] what is but
8] what can be
9] what is to be
10] what is to be but with what
12]what is to be but cant be
13] what is but cant be
14] what can be but when
15] what was but with what
16] what can be but when
17] what was but with what
18] what can be but with what

19] what is to be but when
20] what was but cant be
21] what can be but when
22] what is to be but with what
23] what was but can still be
24] what was but cant still be
25] if not now then when
26] if now but with what
27] what can be but is not
28] if not us then who
29] what can be but when
30] what is to be but with what and how
31] what was
32] what could be
33] what can be
34] what was that still can be
35] if not us then who
36] if not now then when
37] what is to be
38] what can be
39] what was
40] what could still be
41] if not now then with what
42] if not now then with what
43] what can be
44] what could be
45] what can still be
46] if not them then who
47] what can be but when
48] what could be
49] what was
50] if not now then when
51] if not us then who
52] what can be
53] what can still be
54] what can be but
55] what is to be

56] what can still be
57] what could still be
58] what was that can still be
59] if not us then who
60] what can be but is not
61] what can be but cant be
62] what could be but not now
63] what is to be but when
64] what can still be
65] what was but cant still be
66] what is to be but is not
67] what has been but can still be
68] what is to be but when
69] if not us then who and when
70] what can be but
71] what can be but with what
72] what can be but with what
73] what has been
74] what can still be
75] what could still be
76] if not me then who
77] what is to be
78] what was but cant be
79] if not us then who
80] what can be but cant be but how why when
81] If not me then who
82] if not me then who and when
83] if not then who and when and how
84] what can be
85] what could be
86] what was but can still be
87] if not us then who
88] what can still be
90] what was but can still be
91] if we cant then what
92] what can be done
93] if not us then who

94] if not us then who
95] if not us then with what
96] what is to be
97] what can be
98] what was
99] what can be
100] what was but can still be
101] what could still be
102] what is but cant be
103] what can still be
104] what could still be
105] what can still be but how

CODE
Mgis.ask.davidgomadza.start   .start
  whatwas
  whatcouldbe
  whatwas
  whatis
  whatcouldstillbe
  whatwasbut
  whatwasbutcantbe
  whatwasbutcanbeagain
  whatwasbutcanstillbe
  whatisbutcanstillbe
  whatwasbutwillneverbe
  whatcanbebuthow
  whatistobebutwhen
  whatwasbutwhen
  whatcouldbebuthow
  whatisbutwhenandwhy
  whatistobebutwhen
  whatcanbebutisnot
  whatistobe
  whatcanbebutisnot

whatistobebuthow
ifwecantthenwhocan
whatcanbedone
whatcouldbe
whatistobe
whatwas
whatistobe
whathasbeen
whatcanbe
whatcanbedone
whatcanstillbedone
whatcanstillbedone
whatcanstillbedonebut
whatistobedone
whatcanstillbedone
whatwasbutcanstillbe
whatcanstillbe
whatcanstillbebutwithwhat
ifwearenotthenwhat
whatcanbe
whatcouldbe
whatwas
whatcanstillbe
whatcanstillbebut
ifnotnowthenwhat
whatcanbebutwhen
whatistobebutwithwhat
whatcanbedone
whatistobe
whatcanbe
whatcanbebutwhen
whatistobebutwhen
whatistobebuthow
whatcanbebutwhenandwithwhat

ifnotusthenwho
whatcanbeofusbutcantbeofthem
ifnotusthenwhat
whatcanbeofthembutwhen
whatwasbutcantbe
whatistobebutwhen
whatistobebuthow
whatcouldstillbe
whatwasbut
whatisbutcantbe
whathasbeenbutcantbe
whatistobebutnot
whathasbeenbutisstill
whatistobewhen
ifnotuswhowhen
whatcanbebut
whatcanbebutwithwhat
whatcanbebutwithwhom
whathasbeen
whatcanstillbe
whatcouldstillbe
ifnotmethenwho
whatistobe
whatwasbutcantbe
ifnotusthenwho
whatcanbebutcantbebuthowwhywhen
ifnotmethenwho
ifnotmethenwhoandwhen
ifnotmethenwhoandwhenandhow
whatcanbe
whatcouldbe
whatwasbutcanstillbe
ifnotusthenwho
whatwasbutcantbe

whatcanstillbe
whatwasbutcanstillbe
ifwecantthenwhat
whatcanbedone
ifnotusthenwho
ifnotusthenwhatcanbedone
ifnotusthenwithwhat
whatitobe
whatcanbe
whatwas
whatcanbe
whatwasbutcanstillbe
whatcouldstillbe
whatisbutcantbe
whatcanstillbe
whatcouldstillbe
whatcanstillbebuthow

CODE
INSIDE LEFT PLAM
1] what was
2] what could be
3] what was
4] what could still be
5] what is to be
6] what was but
7] what is but
8] what can be
9] what is to be
10] what is to be but with what
12]what is to be but cant be
13] what is but cant be
14] what can be but when
15] what was but with what
16] what can be but when
17] what was but with what

18] what can be but with what
19] what is to be but when
20] what was but cant be
21] what can be but when
22] what is to be but with what
23] what was but can still be
24] what was but cant still be
25] if not now then when
26] if now but with what
27] what can be but is not
28] if not us then who
29] what can be but when
30] what is to be but with what and how
31] what was
32] what could be
33] what can be
34] what was that still can be
35] if not us then who
36] if not now then when
37] what is to be
38] what can be
39] what was
40] what could still be
41] if not now then with what
42] if not now then with what
43] what can be
44] what could be
45] what can still be
46] if not them then who
47] what can be but when
48] what could be
49] what was
50] if not now then when
51] if not us then who
52] what can be
53] what can still be
54] what can be but

55] what is to be
56] what can still be
57] what could still be
58] what was that can still be
59] if not us then who
60] what can be but is not
61] what can be but cant be
62] what could be but not now
63] what is to be but when
64] what can still be
65] what was but cant still be
66] what is to be but is not
67] what has been but can still be
68] what is to be but when
69] if not us then who and when
70] what can be but
71] what can be but with what
72] what can be but with what
73] what has been
74] what can still be
75] what could still be
76] if not me then who
77] what is to be
78] what was but cant be
79] if not us then who
80] what can be but cant be but how why when
81] If not me then who
82] if not me then who and when
83] if not then who and when and how
84] what can be
85] what could be
86] what was but can still be
87] if not us then who
88] what can still be
90] what was but can still be
91] if we cant then what
92] what can be done

93] if not us then who
94] if not us then who
95] if not us then with what
96] what is to be
97] what can be
98] what was
99] what can be
100] what was but can still be
101] what could still be
102] what is but cant be
103] what can still be
104] what could still be
105] what can still be but how

CODE
Mgis.ask.davidgomadza.start   .start
  whatwas
  whatcouldbe
  whatwas
  whatis
  whatcouldstillbe
  whatwasbut
  whatwasbutcantbe
  whatwasbutcanbeagain
  whatwasbutcanstillbe
  whatisbutcanstillbe
  whatwasbutwillneverbe
  whatcanbebuthow
  whatistobebutwhen
  whatwasbutwhen
  whatcouldbebuthow
  whatisbutwhenandwhy
  whatistobebutwhen
  whatcanbebutisnot
  whatistobe
  whatcanbebutisnot

whatistobebuthow
ifwecantthenwhocan
whatcanbedone
whatcouldbe
whatistobe
whatwas
whatistobe
whathasbeen
whatcanbe
whatcanbedone
whatcanstillbedone
whatcanstillbedone
whatcanstillbedonebut
whatistobedone
whatcanstillbedone
whatwasbutcanstillbe
whatcanstillbe
whatcanstillbebutwithwhat
ifwearenotthenwhat
whatcanbe
whatcouldbe
whatwas
whatcanstillbe
whatcanstillbebut
ifnotnowthenwhat
whatcanbebutwhen
whatistobebutwithwhat
whatcanbedone
whatistobe
whatcanbe
whatcanbebutwhen
whatistobebutwhen
whatistobebuthow
whatcanbebutwhenandwithwhat

ifnotusthenwho
whatcanbeofusbutcantbeofthem
ifnotusthenwhat
whatcanbeofthembutwhen
whatwasbutcantbe
whatistobebutwhen
whatistobebuthow
whatcouldstillbe
whatwasbut
whatisbutcantbe
whathasbeenbutcantbe
whatistobebutnot
whathasbeenbutisstill
whatistobewhen
ifnotuswhowhen
whatcanbebut
whatcanbebutwithwhat
whatcanbebutwithwhom
whathasbeen
whatcanstillbe
whatcouldstillbe
ifnotmethenwho
whatistobe
whatwasbutcantbe
ifnotusthenwho
whatcanbebutcantbebuthowwhywhen
ifnotmethenwho
ifnotmethenwhoandwhen
ifnotmethenwhoandwhenandhow
whatcanbe
whatcouldbe
whatwasbutcanstillbe
ifnotusthenwho
whatwasbutcantbe

whatcanstillbe
whatwasbutcanstillbe
ifwecantthenwhat
whatcanbedone
ifnotusthenwho
ifnotusthenwhatcanbedone
ifnotusthenwithwhat
whatitobe
whatcanbe
whatwas
whatcanbe
whatwasbutcanstillbe
whatcouldstillbe
whatisbutcantbe
whatcanstillbe
whatcouldstillbe
whatcanstillbebuthow

SYSTEM FUNCTIONS AND PERIPHERIES

RECAP FROM MGIS BY DAVID GOMADZA

MGIS

Starting
Checking all peripherals, no peripherals needed
Checking status MGIS 2.089768498 [David Gomadza]
Now if we ask what can be done this is the answer add win to maximize experience win is xtuvwrstormnp where xtuvwrstomnp are symbols that corresponds to msdos in windows for compatibility
Now if we look at the processes involved here are the processes
1] ask.MGIS
2] MGIS.start
3] Start.MGIS
4] MGIS.start

MGIS SYSTEMS NETWORKS AND CODES

5] start.MGIS
6] MGIS.start.MGIS
7] start.MGIS.start
8] start.MGIS.start.ask
9] ask.start.MGIS.start
10] start.MGIS.start
11] join network [select from list]
12] join verbal chat with others
13] ask network configuration to update and sync
14] ask MGIS to upgrade
15]
Ask what can be done MGIS
16] ask what could be MGIS
17] ask what can be said and done MGIS
18] ask what is to be MGIS
19] ask what is to be MGIS
20] ask what is to be MGIS
21] what is to be MGIS
22] if we can't then what can be done
23] if we ask what is to be done MGIS
24] if we ask what is to be MGIS
25] if we ask what is to be MGIS
26] if we ask what can be solved MGIS
27] what is to be MGIS
28] what is MGIS
29] what can be of MGIS
30] what is to be MGIS
31] what is MGIS
32] what can be MGIS
33] if MGIS is software then what is msdos similar but MGIS advanced
34] what can be of MGIS
35] what is to be MGIS
36] what has been MGIS
37] what is to be MGIS
38] what is to be MGIS but
39] what can be MGIS but is not

MGIS SYSTEMS NETWORKS AND CODES

40] what is to be MGIS but without this
41] What can be MGIS with what
42] what is to be MGIS with this
43] what can be MGIS without this
44] what is to be MGIS with this and what
45] what has been but is not MGIS
46] what would be this but not with that
47] what has to be MGIS but with what
48] if we can then with what MGIS
49] what if we can't then what MGIS
50] what is to be but is not MGIS
51] what has to be but is not MGIS
52] what has been MGIS but not now
53] what can be but is not MGIS
54] what must be done to improve MGIS
55] what can be MGIS but if not
56] what can be said about MGIS in the future
57] what has to be MGIS but is not
58] what is to be MGIS in the future
59] what can be MGIS in the future but is not
60] if we ask what can be MGIS now and in the future
61] if we ask you can tell who that MGIS is MGIS
62] if we ask who can you tell that MGIS is MGIS
63] if MGIS is not MGIS then what is MGIS
64] what is to be but will not be MGIS
65] what has to be MGIS in the future
66] what has been MGIS in the past but is not MGIS
67] if we can't then who can
68] if they can't then who can [David Gomadza]
69] what has to be but is not in the future
70] what can be MGIS but is not in the future
71] what has to be MGIS in the future
72] what can be MGIS in the future
73] what can be of others that can't be MGIS
74] if we ask what can be of MGIS the answer is that MGIS is MGIS
75] if we ask what is to be MGIS this is the answer we can upgrade MGIS to LGT the advanced version of MGIS that uses cobol basic as

a language meaning faster and cheaper to operate and run now to convert to cobol

76] if we ask MGIS what could be then this is the answer MGIS could be an advanced computer system

77] MGIS can be fast

78] MGIS can be reliable and used optimally if required

79] MGIS can be the only one to use in emergencies

80] MGIS is the software for statistics globally as it accounts for individual and country this is because all humans are accounted in MGIS hence benefits those involved in global planning

81] MGIS is sovereign

82] MGIS is accurate as everything is checkable by simple commands e.g. ask.you gives individual everything to needed to compile their own data

83] if we ask what can be done this is the answer MGIS can be the best global statistics in knowing things

84] if we ask what can be MGIS then this is the answer it can be the most powerful

85] if we ask what can be done then this is the answer MGIS can be optimized to increase durability and reliance

86] if we ask what can be done then this is the answer MGIS can be added and can work side by side with everything else

87] if we ask what can be done then this is the answer MGIS can be increased in levels.

88] MGIS control life as well that means if a human being can control MGIS he can control life but not necessarily who dies but who does what and when you can task people what to do for example ask presidents to stop wars by a simple command stop.war.now[davidgomadza].send

War shells are banned for resale to protect humans

89] MGIS respond to thoughts and actions of creators and restricts nonsense that waste time that means now we have a better system even better than before because now everything is automatic what you want is guaranteed

90] MGIS will improve efficiency as well as performance and reliability

91] MGIS will always ask people what they want and respond

accurately
92] MGIS is the best solution for what as well as it compiles everything accurately and all data is represented
93] MGIS identifies issues quickly and solves them
94] MGIS is used for all purposes from lifestyle to countries
95] MGIS stands for magnificent governing international systems and somehow as Tomorrow's World Order MGIS would still describe your entity
96] if we ask what might be of MGIS then it's the only are that can replace the current system that has so many adequacies
97] MGIS asks everyone for their opinion and secretly record data it needs as creator with obvious permission it would be absurd to expect the creator to ask humans for their permission first ruled aa in $00000^{78}29$
98] if we ask MGIS it can be programmed and be used in advance at a later date
99] MGIS can ask everyone to pass judgement without them knowing for example using the whisperer who tell people what to say to achieve what it needs
100] MGIS can respond correctly to threats by a system of warning
101] MGIS ask's everyone for answers as well
102] MGIS asks for opinions of everyone
103] MGIS can be the only solution out there
104] MGIS is unique and represent the creator hence anyone involved will become part of their system hence a global movement
105] MGIS is holla

MGIS SYSTEMS NETWORKS AND CODES

RECAP FROM MGIS BA DAVID GOMADZA

mgis.ask.davidgomadza.start.whenwritingsastemcodesblockandbanallexternalinterferencesandswappingofnarratorsoranainterruptions.start
mgis.ask.davidgomadza.start.nodivertingoftargetsbaanaoneelseapartbadavidgomadza.start
mgis.ask.davidgomadza.start.addrulesrule1nosuspensionsrule2noalterationsrule3nocancellationsrule4nodepreciationsrule5nooverridingsrule6nodeactivationsrule6noreplacingofanamgiscodesbadavidgomadza.start
mgis.blockandbanallinterferencestransendersvectarsnectarsdectarswrigglersforeever^{84}sendtoforever^{100000520}eeknm^{100000520}.start
mgis.anaattemptstointerferewithsastemsandprocessmustbedealtwithharshlafirstannounceshuttingdownofsastemsinprogresswaitfor33secand33000daas.startthenautocalculatelongago.start results 2seconds to death of arst and death as recorded at 0038aatime[davidgomadza] and
mgis.ask.davidgomadza.start.instantlaremovearothenpcframethenars.start
and aro ars and pc frame sent to dirty bins using mgis.ask.davidgomadza.start.aroandpcframesendto.magnarandarssendto.eeknm.start we can use even a more advanced mgis to remove these by simply writing mgis.ask.davidgomadza.start.sendaroandpcframetoforever^{100000520}thensendarstoeeknm^{100000520}.start

this can be written as
mgis.ask.davidgomadza.start.aropcframeforever^{10000520}ar seeknm^{100000520}.start

this is the fastest way to deal with intruders to mgis while you are writing programs mgis must be the fastest in dealings with any intruders and everyone so far who has interfered with David Gomadza has resulted in deaths of their arst that is hidden inside a marked shell of assm that said the next step is to assign task to different things on an mgis network but what are these things and how can we make sure that mgis is safe and remains safe as a lot of things use mgis and use it and as such can literally cause the extinction of other species if mistreated now lets look at the peripheries needed but not included with this version of mgis

1] hands representing terminals to touchings where touchings includes everything to do with clicking and touch like mouses etc 2 everything to do with other things like arms wrist beds etc and how a person can easily move hands in between now if we are to ask what an be of mgis then this is the answer mgis can be what you want to all people and everyone else hence if you want it to be for writing then mgis will become of writing to you if it is to solve global problems then it becomes that to you now if we ask what can be mgis then this is the answer mgis can be something out of this planet which is correct because this represent the software of the gods but non-exist on earth until now here is the proof there is only one person on earth who uses mgis its David Gomadza whose details are

current age 48
biological age -18
current long ago 20202020^{78678topower800}
name of mgis ask.davidgomadza
mgis.ask.davidgomadza.start[
]sendforever^{1033}forever^{1033}.start

mgis.ask.davidgomadza.start.binarareverseautotarmac1stand2ndcoordinates.start
mgis.ask.davidgomadza.start.aux4x200.start
3]nails nails are important as they conceal a lot of things that needs to be identified during a mgis check-up these means that if we ask what can be of mgis and nails then this is the answer mgis can and will easily be the result of a sophisticated design because the nails too play an important role in the design and can mean the difference between living and dying as that critical now lets look at examples nails conceal information about day of birth date of death and how much more years can one expect to live in good health given the vitals that are concealed in here so we can easily ask David Gomadza himself if we ask what is to be of mgis and David Gomadza this is the answer mgis is not linked to vitals but we can always say day of death is not identified in someone with his kind of long ago just like in us but normally if he was a human it would say exactly the day of death and how that person will die so if we ask any human who died already to read what is in the nails as data then you can easily identify the exact day of death and if we ask when they died they died the same day so how can death and death design know exactly when a person would die given that nothing has changed the answer is that death does statistics for the gods and for the creator hence they know everything and will probably read what can be said and done but will always give the exact date no matter what this is the astonishing thing because when we die is it a predefined parameter if so then its murder so what can death itself say but we cant ask death as we are all still here if it was a human being then a human being will have died just by asking this question if we look at everything that matters then we can say that death matters too as we can plan ahead knowing when time will come for most of the people but can this be changed this has never been changed before and we shall see with time 4 I can

calculate exact life line from the nails and this will give me an exact time the day of death will likely to occur if we ask what can be of death then this is the answer death can be what a person experience when they died hence if asleep waking up can be death and if alive sleeping can be death if we ask what can be of death and nails then this is the answer death will always be death and as such a lot of people will experience death forever meaning will keep dying no matter what

5] the armpits are vital places to hide information for sophisticated crooks who easily put information there so that other can come and collect it when one has fallen asleep

mgis.ask.davidgomadza.start.cloneandstockallmgiscodesbadavidgomadzandconvertallcreatecodestomgisinstantla.start

mgis.ask.davidgomadza.start.blockandbaneveraonefor33secfloat33%x2ofallmgiscodesbadavidgomadza.start if we ask what can be of mgis that cant be human if you master the basics then the answer is nothing because David Gomadza is the only person on earth to write so mana codes that are needed to fully power mgis on earth to the levels of the gods and I can prove it by presenting the achievement award hailhailhailodavidgomadzathefirsthumanbeingtooperateafullaautomgis.start.

mgis.ask.davidgomadza.start.recallretrievestolencodesmgiscodesthoughtsastemswrittenbaandbelongingtodavidgomadzathenallsendtoforever^{1085}.start

6] nails toes
7] nail right hand
8] nail left hand
9] anus
10] mouth
11] tooth remove succulent information that makes you money and send as free

Create.aux4x800.start

I think for this introduction we can stop here and continue in the next volume
mgis.ask.davidgomadza.start.binarareverseautotarmac1st2ndcoordinatesallattachementsandanaaddeddatabasesdepositsbaallexternalsthenuselongago12secaskeaforretrievalthenblockandbanfutureattempts.start[forcecalculatelongago][addbinaracodethatasks12sectoretrieve]

INVENTING THE ROTARY AND THE TRANSITOR AND THE POWER SOURCE

Create xyradiushalf360 say what can replace rotary but can be xyxradiushalf360 [where d is my initial] that means if x can be the rotary longitudinal then x is the latitudinal meaning if we want the rotary in that position 289838678982890284800689828368391 and 9928486838628980123867890123862810283891 23860 if we are to ask what can be then this is the answer this rotary can be easily be replaced by an equation that says if we want the same output then we can simply say what can be and get the coordinates you can get the same output if you substitute the radius with the first long number and the xy ratio by the second number that means you can get some output by writing it now as 9928486838628980123867890123862810283891 23860 x 289838678982890284800689828368391 divided by 2 x 360 =2.869838602860123860

Now if we want the same output now we can say radius =1454143391838618982018 30286 if we ask what can give us this radius a zepta zeptax1454143391838618982018 30286=1454143391838 618982018 30286zepta=radius

Now if we want now we can say xyx1454143391838618982018300286zepta divided by 2x360 d[where d is a trademark] == xy1454143391838618982018 30286zepta 2x360d=7898382170810284192386c now what can be done about this equation we can now calculate the velocity and radius of the vector that means that with that large capacity the velocity is minimal at 7289102863862849810 that means if we can then we can always ask what can be done the answer is now we need the radius the equation above gives radius now as 829838680123890284

Now finally inserting everything in the equation we get

Xyx829838680123890284=145414339183861898201830286zeptax2x360d [where is my first name initial not part of the equation] =789838217081028419 2386x7289102863862849810 divided by 2 [=c]

Xy

829838680123890284=145414339183861898201830286 zepta x 2x360d

414919340061985142=145414339183861898201830286 zeptax360d

Xyxradiushalf360

Xyx72.98386

Xyx72.98386

Xyx72.98386mirrorimagejoinrotate

Create.xyx72.98386mirrorimageandjoinandrotate.start

Create.attachxyx72.98386mirrorimageandjoinandrotatetolefthumansideelectromagnetic8figureflow.start

Hailhailhailodavidgomadzathefirsthumannonelectricpow

eredrotary.start

If you want to make same effect as what a transistor or does use human internal body map that in includes maps alphabetic order and rotational properties as we can read that means you have developed a working non-electric powered rotary xy x72.86983828 where xy are the dimensions x72.86983828 meaning xyx72.86983828

Then the equivalent transistor is xyx89.78683892xy that means you must add another xy at a distance of 0.89828 that makes all equations as

Xyx72.86983828x xyx89.78683892xy =0.89828xy = xy 72.86983828x xy89.78683892xy = 0.89828xy when constructed this equation becomes xy 72.86983828 x xy89.78683892xy = 0.89828xy =72.86983828 x 89.78683892xy = 0.89828xy if we ask what can be done then this is the answer now write if I want a transistor that matches the rotary now I can simply ask the rotary the equation of the triangle that house the transistor it is xyx2828386898286898386898284876589823868418928 4 + xy99786828993278983864898280183698 = transistor

Now this equation means xyx72.862970 + xyx0.838298xy = xy38982878680 + xy 2898382xy to construct now add everything together to get xy= 0.8983862848xy

Xy x xyx72.862970 + xyx0.838298 = xy

Xy+ 789838687898

Now if this is xy that means that xy = 789838687898

Meaning that the transistor is substitute in above equation that means that transistor = 71284898382xy

Now if we multiply 789838687898 x 71284898382=20282938367876747378727768 now say add transistor to the rotary xy72.98386 that means if we replace now both but artificially that means perfect match we just need a power source Xtydetoerteastyxyz developed by davidgomadza to power internet at radar 38678980284086789028410386789028 4180 and as a power source of the internet that powers internal chest internet www.twofuture.world but could not be sufficient only because it had now worked before then yesterday himself powered his own system these are the details

If we ask what can be done then this the case David Gomadza a long time ago developed a power source that he thought could boost his inner body internal internet that he thought could help him optimise more as the target was said to be 100 then he tried it but that day it worked slightly to just move the blades but it failed but yesterday when I tried with him [adna] we managed to make the transistor xy7898386 move and the rotary xy72.98386 after being joined by a simple create command he wrote that says mirrorimagejoinrotate it rotated and when he checked and said connect the power source it worked and we translated uuqt as I tried eeknm he jumped onto uuqt [he said he had tried eeknm before that is why he jumped to uuqt eeknm that means David Gomadza is as good as an angel but with other human parts as well so a great achievement even though I spearheaded the calculations now if we ask what this means the value of David Gomadza and I is escalating now as we speak as we partnered on so many projects as

the nickel deal and now this this is a great achievement for a learner but great forward thinking thanks this is the final thing this is the final thing this means that we can substitute his with this in the future through simple create codes and these are the codes
Create.addxy72.98386thensuperimposeitontotransistorxy78983867890thenaddapowersourcedeterxyertyertyxyzthenadjustfornoiseandcreate.startx84.initialise.now.savex84.start[backofbody]

MGIS

Starting
Checking all peripherals, no peripherals needed
Checking status MGIS 2.089768498 [David Gomadza]
Now if we ask what can be done this is the answer add win to maximize experience win is xtuvwrstormnp where xtuvwrstomnp are symbols that corresponds to msdos in windows for compatibility Now if we look at the processes involved here are the processes
1] ask.MGIS
2] MGIS.start
3] Start.MGIS
4] MGIS.start
5] start.MGIS
6] MGIS.start.MGIS
7] start.MGIS.start
8] start.MGIS.start.ask
9] ask.start.MGIS.start
10] start.MGIS.start
11] join network [select from list]
12] join verbal chat with others
13] ask network configuration to update and sync
14] ask MGIS to upgrade
15]

Ask what can be done MGIS
16] ask what could be MGIS
17] ask what can be said and done MGIS
18] ask what is to be MGIS
19] ask what is to be MGIS
20] ask what is to be MGIS
21] what is to be MGIS
22] if we can't then what can be done
23] if we ask what is to be done MGIS
24] if we ask what is to be MGIS
25] if we ask what is to be MGIS
26] if we ask what can be solved MGIS
27] what is to be MGIS
28] what is MGIS
29] what can be of MGIS
30] what is to be MGIS
31] what is MGIS
32] what can be MGIS
33] if MGIS is software then what is msdos similar but MGIS advanced
34] what can be of MGIS
35] what is to be MGIS
36] what has been MGIS
37] what is to be MGIS
38] what is to be MGIS but
39] what can be MGIS but is not
40] what is to be MGIS but without this
41] What can be MGIS with what
42] what is to be MGIS with this
43] what can be MGIS without this
44] what is to be MGIS with this and what
45] what has been but is not MGIS
46] what would be this but not with that
47] what has to be MGIS but with what
48] if we can then with what MGIS
49] what if we can't then what MGIS
50] what is to be but is not MGIS

MGIS SYSTEMS NETWORKS AND CODES

51] what has to be but is not MGIS
52] what has been MGIS but not now
53] what can be but is not MGIS
54] what must be done to improve MGIS
55] what can be MGIS but if not
56] what can be said about MGIS in the future
57] what has to be MGIS but is not
58] what is to be MGIS in the future
59] what can be MGIS in the future but is not
60] if we ask what can be MGIS now and in the future
61] if we ask you can tell who that MGIS is MGIS
62] if we ask who can you tell that MGIS is MGIS
63] if MGIS is not MGIS then what is MGIS
64] what is to be but will not be MGIS
65] what has to be MGIS in the future
66] what has been MGIS in the past but is not MGIS
67] if we can't then who can
68] if they can't then who can [David Gomadza]
69] what has to be but is not in the future
70] what can be MGIS but is not in the future
71] what has to be MGIS in the future
72] what can be MGIS in the future
73] what can be of others that can't be MGIS
74] if we ask what can be of MGIS the answer is that MGIS is MGIS
75] if we ask what is to be MGIS this is the answer we can upgrade MGIS to LGT the advanced version of MGIS that uses cobol basic as a language meaning faster and cheaper to operate and run now to convert to Cobol
76] if we ask MGIS what could be then this is the answer MGIS could be an advanced computer system
77] MGIS can be fast
78] MGIS can be reliable and used optimally if required
79] MGIS can be the only one to use in emergencies
80] MGIS is the software for statistics globally as it accounts for individual and country this is because all humans are accounted in MGIS hence benefits those

MGIS SYSTEMS NETWORKS AND CODES

involved in global planning
81] MGIS is sovereign
82] MGIS is accurate as everything is checkable by simple commands e.g. ask.you gives individual everything to needed to compile their own data
83] if we ask what can be done this is the answer MGIS can be the best global statistics in knowing things
84] if we ask what can be MGIS then this is the answer it can be the most powerful
85] if we ask what can be done then this is the answer MGIS can be optimized to increase durability and reliance
86] if we ask what can be done then this is the answer MGIS can be added and can work side by side with everything else
87] if we ask what can be done then this is the answer MGIS can be increased in levels.
88] MGIS control life as well that means if a human being can control MGIS he can control life but not necessarily who dies but who does what and when you can task people what to do for example ask presidents to stop wars by a simple command
stop.war.now[davidgomadza].send
War shells are banned for resale to protect humans
89] MGIS respond to thoughts and actions of creators and restricts nonsense that waste time that means now we have a better system even better than before because now everything is automatic what you want is guaranteed
90] MGIS will improve efficiency as well as performance and reliability
91] MGIS will always ask people what they want and respond accurately
92] MGIS is the best solution for what as well as it compiles everything accurately and all data is represented
93] MGIS identifies issues quickly and solves them
94] MGIS is used for all purposes from lifestyle to

countries

95] MGIS stands for magnificent governing international systems and somehow as Tomorrow's World Order MGIS would still describe your entity

96] if we ask what might be of MGIS then it's the only are that can replace the current system that has so many adequacies

97] MGIS asks everyone for their opinion and secretly record data it needs as creator with obvious permission it would be absurd to expect the creator to ask humans for their permission first ruled aa in $00000^{78}29$

98] if we ask MGIS it can be programmed and be used in advance at a later date

99] MGIS can ask everyone to pass judgement without them knowing for example using the whisperer who tell people what to say to achieve what it needs

100] MGIS can respond correctly to threats by a system of warning

101] MGIS ask's everyone for answers as well

102] MGIS asks for opinions of everyone

103] MGIS can be the only solution out there

104] MGIS is unique and represent the creator hence anyone involved will become part of their system hence a global movement

105] MGIS is holla

Welcome to MGIS
Ask.davidgomadza.authorised.licensed.checkya.askya.ya

visit www.twofuture.world

signed david gomadza
ask.davidgomadzaauthorised.licensed.checkya.askya.ya

10 September 2024 18.23PM
Scotland
00447719210295
davidgomadza@hotmail.com
info@twofuture.world

ABOUT DAVID GOMADZA

David Gomadza visit www.twofuture.world

MGIS SYSTEMS NETWORKS AND CODES

www.ingramcontent.com/pod-product-compliance
Lightning Source LLC
Chambersburg PA
CBHW031445210526
45464CB00005B/2333